FORCES AND MOVEMENT

Peter Riley

W

FRANKLIN WATTS

NEW YORK • LONDON • SYDNEY

First published in 1998 by
Franklin Watts
96 Leonard Street,
London
EC2A 4RH

Franklin Watts Australia
14 Mars Road
Lane Cove
NSW 2066

Series editor: Sarah Snashall
Editor: Janet De Saulles
Art director: Robert Walster

Designer: Mo Choy
Picture research: Sue Mennell
Photography: Steve Shott
(unless otherwise credited)
Artwork: Sean Wilkinson

A CIP catalogue record for
this book is available from
the British Library.

ISBN 0 7496 2962 2

Dewey classification 531

Printed in Belgium

Picture credits:
Cover and title page Robert
Harding/I Tomlinson
Eye Ubiquitous pp. 4t (P. Seheult)
Getty Images pp. 5l (T. Duffy), 6t
(D. Madison), 8r (N. Parfitt), 12t
(M. Dalmasso), 17t (P. Cole), 20m
(M. Goddard), 20b, 22 (G. Fisher),
23 (D. Higgs); Image Bank pp. 5r,
18t (J. P. Kelly), 19t (Yellow Dog
Prods), 26b (A. Rosario),
28t (P. Loven); Image Select pp. 7t
(Allsport), 9t, 14b (Allsport);
Images p.13t; Kos Picture Source
Ltd/C. Borlenghi p.20t; Planet
Earth Pictures pp. 8l (S. P Hopkin);
Rex Features p.6b; Science Photo
Library pp. 16b (Nasa), 26t (Dale
Boyer/Nasa);Telegraph Colour
Library pp. 16t (T Zimmermann),
17b, 21, 27;
The Stock Market pp. 28b, 29

CONTENTS

PUSHING AND PULLING

A force is a push or a pull. You cannot see a force, but you can see and feel its effects. You see the effect of the wind's force as leaves move on a tree, or feel its effect as the air pushes against your skin.

EXERTING FORCES

The word *exerted* is used to describe how a force is made. We say that wind exerts a force when it blows the leaves. You exert a force on this page when you turn it.

Pushes and pulls move things. Once something is moving, a pull or a push may be exerted to change its direction and speed – or to stop it altogether. For example, you may use a bat to change the direction of a ball that is thrown to you.

The force of the wind is making the seats of these deckchairs billow.

These children are using their muscles, exerting a force to pick up this heavy box.

MOVEMENT

Without forces there would be no movement. When muscles work, they exert forces that pull on your bones and move your limbs, letting you run, walk and swim. Engines exert forces to move cars, trucks, ships, submarines and spacecraft.

ENERGY

The power to exert forces comes from energy. Your muscles get their energy from the food that you eat. Engines get their energy from fuels such as petrol or diesel.

The people on this fairground ride are feeling lots of pulls and pushes. What do you think they are?

The engine is pushing the dragster along at great speed.

INVESTIGATE!

Work out when you are pushing and pulling. Begin by closing this book and opening it again. When did you push? When did you pull? Try other activities and decide when you are pushing and pulling.

GRAVITY

All large objects in space, such as the Earth, have gravity. This is a force which they exert and which pulls other objects towards their surface. The larger the size of the object, the stronger the force of gravity.

THE PULL OF GRAVITY

You feel the effect of gravity if you lose your balance – you fall over! If you throw a ball up into the air, the force you exert pushes the ball up. The ball continues to rise until the effect of gravity becomes stronger than the force of your throw. Gravity pulls the ball downwards towards the Earth.

This gymnast has lost her balance and gravity has pulled her to the ground.

The force of gravity pulls the diver towards the water's surface.

THROWING AND CATCHING

If you throw a ball horizontally, it does not move in a straight line through the air. As it travels forwards, it goes lower and lower until it hits the ground. Gravity pulls on the ball and makes it fall.

For this reason, when you throw a ball to a friend, you usually throw the ball upwards in the direction of your friend. If you have thrown the ball high enough and hard enough, gravity will pull the ball down in time for your friend to catch it.

A tennis player has to hit the ball hard so that it travels over the net before falling towards the ground.

These children are having fun judging how hard and how high to throw the ball to each other.

INVESTIGATE!

Throw a ball to a friend. Keep moving further apart and throwing the ball to each other. See how high you have to throw the ball for each of you to catch it.

WEIGHT

Everything around you, as well as you yourself, is made of a substance called matter. Matter may be a solid, such as rock, a liquid, such as water, or a gas, such as oxygen. The amount of matter in something is called its mass. The force of gravity pulls down on the mass of the solid, liquid or gas and gives it a force called weight. The weight presses down on the Earth.

WEIGHT AND MASS

The weight of something depends on its mass. An object with a small amount of mass has a small weight. An object with a large amount of mass has a large weight.

A ladybird is so light you can hardly feel it as it walks across your skin.

The African elephant has the greatest mass of all land animals – and the greatest weight!

WEIGHT AND GRAVITY

Because the Moon is smaller than the Earth, it has a smaller force of gravity. When astronauts visit the Moon, they weigh six times less than they do on Earth. They still have the same mass as they had on Earth because their bodies do not change. Only the pulling force of gravity has changed.

In space, the force of gravity does not pull this astronaut down. His jetpack, or Manned Manoeuvring Unit (MMU), provides the force he needs to move.

USING A BALANCE

The weight of two different things can be compared by using a balance. The two objects are placed on the trays of the balance: if the objects have the same weight, each end is pushed down with the same force and the balance stays horizontal. If one object weighs more than the other, it pushes more strongly on the balance than the other object and the balance becomes tilted.

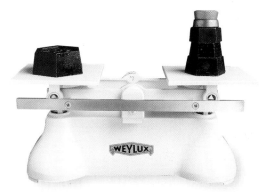

The weights on this balance weigh the same amount, so the balance is horizontal.

INVESTIGATE!

Hang a wire coat-hanger on a bar. Now tie two empty yogurt pots of the same size to its ends. Put an object in each pot. Can you find two objects which weigh the same, so the coat-hanger stays horizontal?

MEASURING FORCE

Springs can be used to measure forces. When a force pulls on a spring, the spring stretches. If the force is made larger, the spring gets longer.

FORCE METERS

A force measurer or force meter is made using a spring, a scale and a pointer. One end of the spring has a hook which attaches to the object exerting the force to be measured. At the other end of the spring is a pointer which moves in front of a scale, showing how much the spring has been stretched by the force.

STRETCHING

Force meters measure small forces by using a weak spring which stretches a large amount when a small force pulls on it. A force meter which measures large forces uses a strong spring. It only stretches a tiny amount when it is pulled by a small force, but stretches greatly when pulled by a large force.

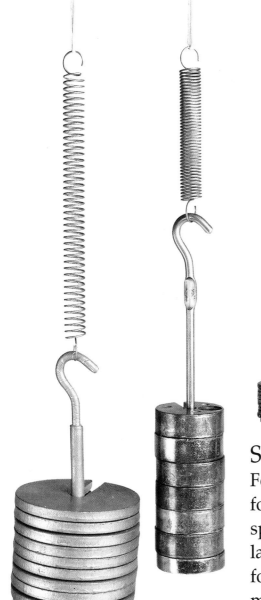

Different weights stretch springs by different amounts.

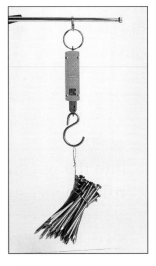

A force meter.

WEIGHING MACHINES

Force meters can be used to measure weight. Weight is a force. In science experiments, the scale on the force meter measures weight in Newtons. Weighing machines such as bathroom and kitchen scales measure weight in kilograms or pounds. The number shown by the pointer on the weighing machine records the amount of matter in an object.

The arrangement of springs in kitchen scales.

Bathroom scales have a spring which is squashed by the weight placed on top of them.

INVESTIGATE!

Make a weighing machine from an elastic band and an empty yogurt pot. Put different objects into the pot and use a ruler to measure how much the elastic band stretches for each object.

BALANCING FORCES

Forces push and pull on objects all the time – even when the object is not moving. The force of gravity pulls on everything on the Earth's surface. Objects or people do not sink into the Earth because there is a force from the Earth's surface pushing back against the force of gravity. The force of gravity is balanced by this pushing force. The result is that the object stays on the Earth's surface.

If the Earth's surface did not push against our weight, we would sink into the ground as if it were wet mud.

TUG OF WAR

Balanced forces can occur in any direction, not just upwards and downwards. If two people are pulling in opposite directions with the same force they do not move.

When one person is stronger, the forces are no longer balanced. The stronger of the two people pulls the other person towards him- or herself.

BRIDGES

A bridge is held up by balanced forces. The weight of a suspension bridge is balanced by forces pushing upwards in the supports and pulling along the cables.

The Golden Gate Bridge, California, is a superb example of a suspension bridge.

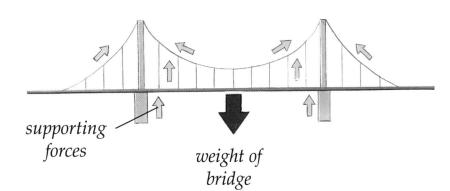

supporting forces

weight of bridge

TENTS

When you put up a tent, the poles are supported by guy ropes which are pegged into the ground. The ropes are tightened so that they pull on the poles. Each rope is placed so that its pulling force on the poles is balanced by the pulling force of the other ropes.

INVESTIGATE!

Make a ruler stand on end by using string and sticky tape 'guy ropes' to hold it up.

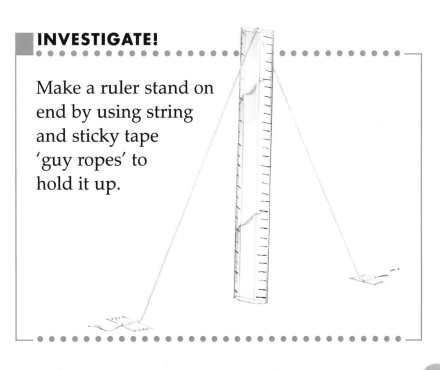

THE CENTRE OF GRAVITY

The weight of a free-standing object pulls down from a point in the object called the centre of gravity. The part of an object which is directly underneath its centre of gravity is called its base.

GRAVITY AND BALANCE

When the weight pulls down from the centre of gravity through the base, the object will not fall over. It is balanced. If an object is tilted too far, it reaches a point where its weight pulls down from the centre of gravity through the object's side, causing it to fall over. The object has lost its balance.

These free-standing objects will not fall over because their weights are pulling down through their bases.

These tilted objects are about to fall over because their weights are pulling down through their sides.

Most cars tilt when they go round a corner fast. Racing cars, however, are built close to the ground. Their weights pull down through their wide bases even when they take corners. This keeps them stable.

Their wide bases help keep racing cars steady.

A skittle has more mass in its lower part than in its upper part, and so is more difficult to knock over than a regularly shaped piece of plastic the same height.

STAYING BALANCED

If an object has more mass in its lower part than in its upper part, its centre of gravity is low – even if the object is tall. This is why it is more difficult to tip over a half-empty bottle than a full one.

Because their weights are pulling down through their sides, the middle blue and red skittles are about to fall over.

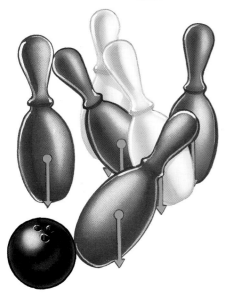

■ INVESTIGATE!

Put some water in the bottom of a plastic bottle, put the lid back on, and see how far you must tip it before it falls over. Try this a few times, adding more water until the bottle is full.

ON THE MOVE

If an object is not moving, the forces acting on it balance. The object's weight is balanced by the upward push from the ground under it. If the object is pushed or pulled from just one end, it starts to move. This is because there is no pushing or pulling force on the other end to balance it.

MOVING IN SPACE

In space, a moving object will keep going in a straight line long after the pushing or pulling force has been removed. If the object passes close to a planet or the Sun, their force of gravity pulls on the object. The force of gravity may pull the object into an orbit.

This bobsleigh team are pushing hard from one end before climbing in to start their run. They are providing the sleigh with the power to make it move.

In 1995, the Galileo spacecraft went into orbit around Jupiter. It released a probe which travelled down to the planet to investigate the conditions there.

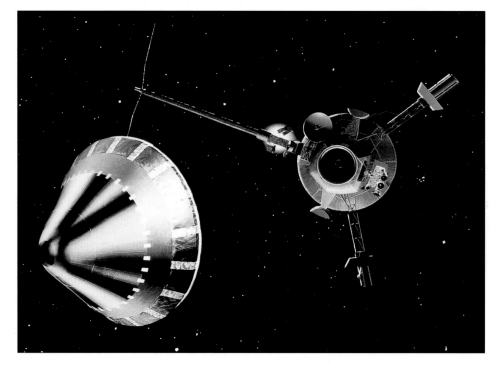

SPEED AND DIRECTION

A moving object can receive extra pulls and pushes. These may make it go faster or slower, or even stop it altogether. It can also be pushed from the side to make it change direction. A stronger force has a greater effect on a moving object than a weaker force. It will make an object speed up or slow down faster – or change direction more quickly – than a weaker force will.

This player has been pushed off the ball as he runs forwards.

As the water is pushed backwards, the boat is pushed forwards.

GOING FORWARD

When you push or pull on something in one direction, a force is exerted in the opposite direction. It is equal in strength to the force you have exerted and is called a reaction force. When someone rows a boat, the oars push the water backwards. A reaction force from the water of the same size, but acting in the opposite direction, pushes the boat forwards.

▌ INVESTIGATE!

Kick a football and run after it. Kick it again to speed it up, then try to slow it down. What force do you use to stop it?

FRICTION

If you put a toy car on the floor, push it and take your hand away, the car will move. But as the car travels across the floor, it slows down and stops. This is due to a force called friction.

SLOWING DOWN

Friction occurs at the places where two objects touch. The friction acting on the toy car occurs between the tyres and the floor, and acts in the opposite direction to the way the car is travelling. When the pushing force to keep the car moving is taken away, the friction force is not balanced and is able to slow down the car.

The thin blades of ice skates reduce the contact between a skater and the ice, allowing the skater to travel quickly.

SMOOTH AND BUMPY SURFACES

If you look closely at the surface of an object, you can see tiny bumps on it. Friction occurs where the bumps of a moving object meet the surface the object is travelling over. The smoother the surface, the more easily things can slide over it.

C

The toy car travelling over the wooden surface (A) is going quicker than the car going over the foam (B). This, in turn, is travelling faster than the car running along the corrugated cardboard (C).

A

B

SKIDDING

Water on a road reduces the friction between the tyres and the road surface and can make cars and other vehicles skid.

Motorbike and car tyres are not smooth. Deep grooves, called the tread, help to spray the water away from the tyre's surface, helping the vehicle to grip the road.

INVESTIGATE!

Find a tray and tip it to make a ramp. Slide small objects such as coins, marbles or rubbers down it. Compare the amount of friction there is between them and the tray.

OIL AND FRICTION

At the axle of a bicycle wheel, metal surfaces rub together. The friction between the surfaces slows down the turning wheel. Oil is used to make a layer to separate the surfaces, reducing the friction and making the wheel turn more easily.

RESISTANCE

A boat moving through water has a force acting against it called water resistance. In a similar way, an object moving through air has a force called air resistance working against it.

The hull of a speed boat is streamlined to reduce water resistance.

AIR RESISTANCE

The shape of a vehicle affects the amount of air resistance, or drag, on the vehicle. Curved surfaces, such as on the body of a sports car, allow the air to flow easily over an object and the air resistance is low.

If the object has got large flat surfaces facing the way the object is moving, such as the surfaces on the front of a truck, the air resistance, or drag, is high.

There is less air resistance pushing on the sports car than on the truck.

The air resistance on the parachute slows down the sky diver's fall.

TRAVELLING AT SPEED

At low speeds, such as walking speed, the force of air resistance is weak. But as the speed of the object increases, air resistance increases too. For this reason, racing cyclists who wish to travel fast wear streamlined helmets, and runners wear skin-tight clothes.

USING AIR RESISTANCE

Air resistance can be used to our advantage. When sky divers jump, gravity pulls them down to the Earth. They open their parachutes to increase the air resistance so they can make a safe landing.

■ INVESTIGATE!

Make two toy parachutes out of cloth, string and weights. Use a larger piece of cloth for one and compare how fast each one falls.

FLOATING AND SINKING

When an object is put in water, two forces are exerted. These are the weight of the object and a force, called upthrust, which comes from the water. The weight pulls the object down. The upthrust pushes upwards on the object.

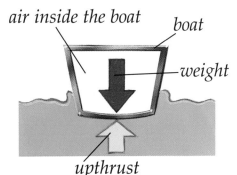

air inside the boat   boat

weight

upthrust

UPTHRUST
When an object is put in water, it pushes some of the water out of the way. The water that has had to move pushes back on the object. The more water pushed away, the greater the upthrust.

Here, the upthrust from the water is stronger than the weight of the boat, so the boat floats.

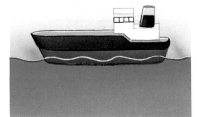

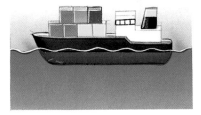

BOATS CONTAIN AIR
A solid block of metal and a boat made of metal may each have the same weight. The solid block, however, will sink while the metal boat will float. This is because the metal boat is shaped into a container and holds a great deal of air. This pushes a larger amount of water out of the way than the block does. The weight of the air and the metal in the boat is less than the upthrust pushing back on the boat, making the boat float.

SUBMARINES

A submarine has large tanks which can be filled with air or water. When the tanks contain air, the submarine floats. When they contain water, the submarine sinks. This is because water weighs more than air. A submarine makes a dive by allowing air out of its tanks and letting water in. It rises from the depths by using compressed air to push the water out from its tanks.

Water enters the tanks, making the submarine dive.

Compressed air pushes the water out of the tanks, making the submarine rise.

INVESTIGATE!

Test which objects float the best. Put some small objects in a bowl of water and see which is pushed furthest out of the water.

ELASTIC BANDS AND SPRINGS

When you stretch an elastic band you can feel it pull against your fingers. The longer you stretch it, the stronger the pulling force you can feel. The band is exerting a force to make itself shorter again.

USING ELASTIC BANDS

An elastic band can be used to keep papers together. The force in a stretched elastic band pushes on the papers and stops them separating. A stretched elastic band can also be used to launch a glider. The elastic band in the glider launcher is connected to a hook on the underside of the glider. When the glider is pulled back, the elastic band stretches. When the glider is released, the pulling force in the elastic band makes the band shorter and pushes the glider into the air.

COIL SPRINGS

Springs are made out of a coil of metal wire. There are two kinds of springs – close coil springs and open coil springs. Close coil springs are designed to be stretched outwards and open coil springs are designed to be squashed inwards.

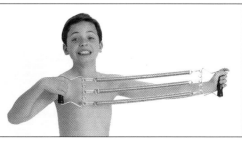

PUSHING AND PULLING

When a close coil spring is stretched, it exerts a pulling force to make itself shorter again. If the stretched spring is released, this pulling force makes the spring shorten very quickly. When an open coil spring is squashed it exerts a pushing force to stretch itself again. If the squashing force is released, the pushing force in the spring makes it stretch back very quickly.

Pulling on the close coil springs of a chest expander helps develop strong chest and arm muscles.

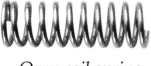

Close coil spring

Open coil spring

INVESTIGATE!

Have a look around your home to find where springs are used. Make a list of all the objects which use open coil springs and all those which use close coil ones.

This punch ball uses a close coil spring at its base.

25

FLIGHT

When an aeroplane moves there are four forces acting on it: thrust, drag, lift and weight. When the thrust force is stronger than the drag force, the aeroplane goes forward. When the lift force is stronger than the weight, the plane moves up.

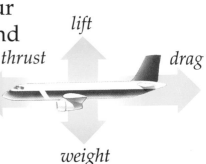

lift

thrust

drag

weight

DRAG
Drag is a force exerted by the air as it rushes over the aeroplane's body. It pulls on the aeroplane to slow it down and stop it. The smoother the surfaces of the plane, the smaller the drag.

THRUST
Thrust is the force exerted by the plane's engines. It moves the craft forward.

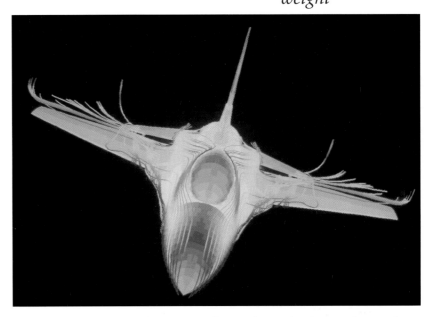

This computerised image of an aircraft shows how the air flows around the plane when it is in flight.

The curve of the wing helps to reduce the drag force exerted on the plane.

LIFT
A wing has a curved upper surface and a flat lower surface. The air moving over the curved surface pushes down on it. The air moving under the flat surface pushes upwards. The upward force is stronger than the downward force so the wing is pushed upwards. This is the force called lift.

WEIGHT

The lift force must be greater than the aeroplane's weight to make the aeroplane take off and stay in the air. The size of the lift force depends on the speed of the air rushing under the wings. The faster the speed, the greater the lift. An aeroplane moves at great speed along a runway. This makes the air rush under its wings so fast that the lift force raises the aeroplane into the air.

The high speed of the aeroplane makes the lift force strong enough for the aeroplane to rise in the air.

INVESTIGATE!

Make a model wing like the one in the picture. Blow from the front of the wing and watch the wing rise up the string.

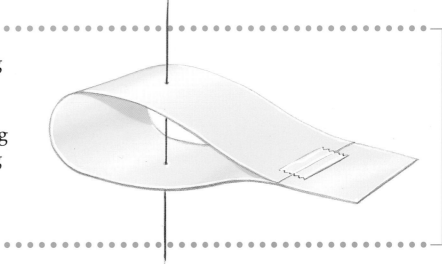

JET ENGINES AND ROCKETS

Most aeroplanes have jet engines to provide thrust, while spacecraft have rocket engines. Both engines make a jet of hot gases which rushes out of the engine at great force. The force of the gases moving backwards is balanced by a force of equal size pushing forwards. This forwards pushing force is the thrust.

The heat inside the jet engine makes it glow.

A huge amount of power is needed to thrust a shuttle from Earth into space.

ENGINES IN SPACE

In a jet engine, fuel called kerosene is used to make the hot gases. Jet engines use oxygen from the air to make this fuel burn.

A rocket engine has to work in space. As there is no air in space, the rocket engine cannot take in oxygen like a jet engine can, and so has to carry its own supply. Although oxygen is a gas, it can be squashed and changed into a liquid, making it easier to store. It is carried on board the craft with the fuel.

CHANGING DIRECTIONS

A spacecraft such as the shuttle orbiter has a number of rocket engines pointing in different directions. Each one can be fired for a short time to change the position of the shuttle, and is used to steer the spacecraft when it is in orbit.

Small rocket engines on the shuttle orbiter are used for steering.

INVESTIGATE!

See how a rocket is provided with the thrust to blast it into space. Stick a straw into an uninflated balloon and run a thread through the straw. Blow up the balloon, release it, and watch it move along the thread as the air comes out.

GLOSSARY

AIR RESISTANCE – the force exerted by the air as a vehicle or object moves against it.

ASTRONAUT – a person who travels and works in space.

AXLE – the centre-pin which a wheel spins round.

BOBSLEIGH – a sledge which can be steered and has a brake. It can be used for racing.

CABLE – a very thick cord made of strands of wire.

COMPRESSED – when something has been squashed very strongly in on itself.

CORRUGATED – a material such as cardboard or iron which has been shaped to have ridges and grooves arranged across it.

DRAG – the force of the air as it rushes over a vehicle. Streamlined vehicles create less drag than vehicles with large flat surfaces.

ENGINE – a machine which provides power to move a vehicle such as a car or a spacecraft.

EXERT – to apply a force.

FRICTION – the force which occurs where two objects touch, and where one or more of the objects is moving. If an object is pushed across a surface, and then the pushing force is taken away, the object will continue to move until the force of friction brings it to a stop.

FUEL – a substance which is burnt to release energy. The energy can be used to make an engine work.

GLIDER – an aircraft which flies but is not equipped with an engine.

GRAVITY – a force exerted by a large body such as the Earth, and which pulls other objects towards its surface.

GUY ROPES – ropes attached to a tent and which help to hold the tent up.

GYMNAST – a person who performs body exercises with speed and control, sometimes using apparatus such as ropes and hoops.

JET ENGINE – an engine which produces a forward thrust on an aircraft by burning fuel using oxygen in the air.

LADYBIRD – a small beetle with a pair of wings, usually coloured black and red, which it folds over its back when it is not flying.

MMU – manned manoeuvring unit. This is a large piece of equipment which is strapped to the back of an astronaut and allows him or her to move around in space outside a spacecraft or space station.

MASS – the amount of matter in something.

MATTER – the substance which all the things around you, whether they are solid, liquid or gas, are made of.

MUSCLE – a fleshy part of the body which can be contracted (made shorter) to pull on bones in order to move them.

NEWTON – a unit which is used by scientists when they are measuring forces.

ORBIT – the path taken by an object in space as it moves round a larger object. For example, satellites orbit, or go round the Earth, and the Earth orbits, or goes round, the Sun.

ROCKET ENGINE – an engine which can produce forward thrust from a spacecraft. It uses fuel and liquid oxygen which is stored on board the spacecraft.

SKY DIVER – a person who jumps out of an aircraft and performs acrobatics as he or she falls part of the way through the sky. The sky diver then opens his or her parachute in order to land safely.

SPACE PROBE – a spacecraft which does not have a crew but which carries equipment to measure conditions in space such as temperature.

STREAMLINED – a shape which allows an object to pass easily through air or water.

SUBMARINE – a special kind of ship which can travel underwater.

SUSPENSION BRIDGE – a bridge supported by cables which are connected to supports at each end of the bridge. This design allows the bridge to be used to span wide rivers.

THRUST – the force which pushes an object or vehicle forwards.

TREAD – the pattern on a bike or car tyre. It helps to spray water on the road away from the tyre's surface, so increasing the amount of friction between the tyre and the road.

UPTHRUST – when an object is put into water, its weight is met by a reaction force from the water called upthrust. The weight pulls the object down and the upthrust pushes the object up.

INDEX